WARRIORS OF LIFE

The Martial Art of Existence

Edited By

Wayne Omura

1 2 3 4 5 6 7 8 9 10

Library of Congress Cataloging-in-Publication Data

Omura, Wayne

Warriors of Life: The Martial Art of Existence/
Edited by Wayne Omura

p. cm.
ISBN 978-1-936955-11-4 (paperback : alk. paper)
1. Martial Arts. 2. Philosophy - Eastern 3. Religion and Spirituality

The paper in this book meets the guidelines for permanence and durability of the Committee on Production Guidelines for Book Longevity of the Council on Library Resources, Inc.

WARRIORS OF LIFE

The Martial Art of Existence

Edited By

Wayne Omura

UNACKNOWLEDGMENTS

It is claimed that nothing new can be known or said or done.

Anything written has already been written.

Every movement has already been performed.

The most original thought is at best an embellishment.

This being so, those aware of the redundancy only aggravate the situation by acknowledging their progenitors.

I myself, being not one voice but many, refuse to confuse the issue further by naming sources that must in turn name sources.

Suffice it to say that these sources do indeed exist and are a part of the endless cycle.

Although acknowledged, they will at least remain nameless.

For the warriors of the heart

Whose inner harmony maintain balance

Whose victories reflect peace.

CONTENTS

EDITOR'S PREFACE

Warriors of Life is the popularized English title of the ancient Chinese classic, Battlefield of Life. The eighteen bamboo-strip bundles (comprising the manuscript) were unearthed in the collapsed cellars of the burnt-out Pochen Monastery ruins. The Tibetan monks had revered and treasured its martial philosophy, eventually adopting and claiming the treatise as their own. However, carbon-dating indicates the bamboo to be of a far more ancient origin, pre-dating even Bodhidharma's (Daruma's, Dat-mor's) trek from India through Tibet and into China by at least one thousand years (making it contemporaneous with the writings of Sun Tzu and Lao Tzu).

With the closure of Tibet by the Chinese communists, many temples have been ransacked and burned. Sacred art and heirlooms, ancient manuscripts and religious documents, icons and treasures have reportedly been either stolen or destroyed. Rumors are that the bamboo-bundle treatise resides in the Swiss vault of a high-ranking military officer. But the official government line is to repudiate such claims. In fact, Chinese authorities deny that the original manuscript even exists—claiming it a western fabrication intended to undermine their cultural integrity.

In any case, despite secular political turmoil, various translations (however flawed) still survive to the present. Warriors of Life being one more version of this exemplary martial classic.

TRANSLATOR'S PREFACE

The various idioms, slang, colloquial expressions, and modern terminology were deemed essential in conveying the spirit of this ancient text.

Tensing Lobsam

PART ONE

PRINCIPLES

"What good is fighting

without an ideal?"

Let no pretense be made:

The way of the warrior is the way of death.

The way of life is not the way of death.

Those who wish to follow life should go no further.

As life and death cannot be mixed,

    neither can the way of life be mixed

        with the way of death.

For death stands alone.

    It vanquishes all.

FATAL EMBRACE

As Death stands firm, calmly awaiting all—

    so too should the warrior stand firm,

    awaiting the movement of his opponents,

    calmly inviting their downfall,

        welcoming them peacefully into the arms of death.

FINALE

To the warrior all of life is merely a preparation for death.

Life is a rehearsal for going beyond.

For this reason the final moment must be met with dignity and
honor—no cowardice or timidity,
no lingering melancholy.

The warrior strides purposefully to engage his doom.

IMMORTALS

The warrior has no death wish. It is not as though he wants to die.

It is simply that he no longer fears that which makes others quake
in their boots.

In fact, he is awed, intrigued, and enticed by death. The true
warrior never feels at home unless death is hovering. For
if life is too peaceful, something seems amiss.

Paradoxically, this fascination with death makes the warrior
seemingly immortal.

Since he lacks the fear of dying, he acts as
though he will always live.

In the heat of a deathly skirmish he appears confident and serene.

DEATH - DEFIERS

Because the true warrior is already dead,
    there is nothing to risk,
        no fear of loss,
            no intimidation.

In life, as in war, he wholeheartedly takes the plunge.
    He holds nothing back.
        He has no trepidation or insecurity.
            He never falters or wavers in his resolve.

For being dead has its virtue.
    It makes one immortal.
        Nothing can affect one's sense of self or well-
        being.

Amidst the battlefield of life, the greatest warriors are
    fearless, for they realize that their eulogies have
        already been spoken. Nothing can be changed,
            for their tombstones have long since been
                engraved and set.

The rest of life is merely "icing on the cake."

The warrior can afford to take a chance,
    because there are no chances to take.

A DEATHLY AIR

Having made a pact with death, the warrior moves

uneasily through life. All who encounter him see

only a ghost. It is difficult to interact. Social

intercourse is minimal. For, from the standpoint

of death, life is all so much playacting:

brief, trivial,

not to be taken seriously.

A stench surrounds the warrior—one of battlefields,

graveyards, rotting corpses.

A warrior wishing to pass unnoticed must conceal

large caches of perfume.

RESURRECTION

A dead man knows no fear.

    Unmoved, he is avoided.

        Moved, and he creates terror.

The warrior is a dead man who,

    wishing always to keep the peace,

        moves only when peace is not possible.

One move,

    one look,

        causes panic and turmoil.

For he is a ghost,

    a zombie returning from the dead.

THE WAY OF DEATH IS THE WAY OF LIFE

Following the way of Death is not a love of death, but rather

it is akin to the affection of a distant, secret admirer—

one who remains at arm's length, hidden and

controlled, and yet who cannot help a few

desultory glances—watching and admiring

while no one is aware.

Having death close at hand in no way devalues life—only our

illusions about life. In fact, the warrior treasures every

moment of life because he knows it may very well be his

last. He treats life respectfully because it can so easily

slip from one's grasp.

Each moment is imbued with meaning. Every action is

significant. Every word is measured.

Moment by moment of a warrior's life is laid down upon a

slowly unraveling scroll. It is a continuing epic saga

that climaxes as the scroll comes to its end.

DAILY RENDEZVOUS

Because each day is the last,

    it is also the first.

Death brings the freshness of birth.

    The condemned man savors his last meal.

    The autumn breeze,

    The smell of fallen leaves,

The crickets chirping in the woodshed.

    The senses spring to life when death is the rendezvous.

A WARRIOR'S FATE

Because the way of the warrior is tragic—

    there is no tragedy.

Because the way of the warrior is deadly—

    there is no question of fate.

Because the warrior stands only by himself

    he is never alone.

Because he is surrounded by death—

    there is no room to mourn.

ACCEPTING LOSS

Because life and death contend,

    and because death always wins,

        life is imbued with continual loss.

Loss, in every form, is an inescapable consequence

    of life.

Rather than mourning,

    the warrior treats every loss as a continual test—

        a preparation, a trial run for going beyond.

To lose is not tragic.

    It is necessary suffering,

        for it paves the way for the ultimate loss.

Without loss we would never value what we have gained,

nor realize that everything we have will

eventually be lost.

For Death is the only beneficiary—

the only surviving heir.

THE ULTIMATE LOSS

Because life is a battle that we must ultimately lose,

    the warrior readies himself for his inevitable defeat.

He practices, all lifelong, the rituals of departure.

    In effect, his entire existence is a solemn attendance

    of his own wake.

The true warrior, having mastered his part in the

    final act, leaves the field with dignity and grace.

DEATH ALWAYS THE VICTOR

Since death is inevitable,

    an alliance with the winning team

        proves profitable and logical.

The warrior takes comfort

    knowing he's playing the sure bet.

LIFE IS WAR

That which lacks, desires to possess.

That which possesses, guards and wants more.

The strong kill and devour the weak.

Strife, competition, domination.

Political, social, intellectual, and physical.

There is no end to the contention because life

is based upon the struggle for survival.

It is the yin and the yang.

There is no escaping the cycle.

THE BATTLEGROUND OF LIFE

Human life is the most gruesome battleground.

It far surpasses the carnage of the most

    brutal animals.

The suffering inflicted is intentional.

The agony is prolonged.

There is no mercy, no chance of pardon.

Man, aware and with conscience, is the only animal

    who kills for sport or profit.

He is also the only animal who kills his own kind.

What does the warrior learn?

He learns to treat human life as the vicious

    battle it has become.

He penetrates the veneer of civilization

and plunders the depths.

He focuses on the true battle behind each

and every scene.

HUNGER

All life is warfare. That which has strives to retain.

That which is lacking strives for fulfillment.

The void is filled. Once filled it is emptied and

    must be filled again. The hungry man dines on

        the spoils of life, is content for a moment, but

        then grows hungry again, and again wants more.

Thus stress and contention are natural to life.

The yin and the yang feed upon one another.

To be a warrior means to be a master of conflict—

    to know when to give, when to take, when to

    advance, when to retreat.

In essence it is the art of harmonious conflict—

    adapting to the circumstances, rolling with

    the punches, flowing with the ever-flowing Tao.

POWER - PLAY

Energy-transfer, in all its forms and manifestations, constitutes

the process of life.

Power is the amassing and wielding of energy.

Because people follow life, they also seek power.

Because the warrior follows death,

he seeks ultimately to abstain.

People shun the way of the warrior because it is a negation

of life and energy. For death renders the mad scrambling

for power—useless and futile.

It is really a matter of choice, of one's fancy, of one's destiny.

But when all is said and done, Death always has its way.

UNTOUCHED

In any venture both good and bad adhere.

It is impossible to go forward and yet remain unsullied.

A little dust must be stirred.

A little mud must stick.

This is the yin and the yang.

This is the nature of life.

The world of the warrior reflects this contrast to the

    extreme. The dregs of society arousing the worst

        emotions——side by side with exemplary figures

            inspiring what is noble and sublime.

There is no escape from this predicament because it

    is inherent to life.

The one, by human nature, entails the other.

But just as the lotus, one can float, untouched, upon

the swamp of life—drawing energy and sustenance

from what is beneath.

YES AND NO

Because life is both yin and yang every individual has a
    dual nature.

Your closest friend is not always loyal.

Your lifelong enemy is not always malign.

Forces contend within every heart,
    pulling this way and that,
        struggling for attention.

The true warrior understands the nature of life.

He is happy with his new love,
    but he knows that love may stray.

He is sympathetic to his foe's downfall,
    because his foe may later become a friend.

Embracing the paradoxical nature of life,
    the warrior can never be fooled.

He accepts the possible and the impossible
    every moment of every day.

PARADOX

In the end, those who seek the trappings of life

will always fail. They will clamor after life,

but will eventually meet death. Their struggle

for power and security will be to no avail.

The warrior, seeking death, is following the secret

path. Shunning the frenetic distraction of life,

he treads the esoteric course.

Paradoxically, what is seemingly the common sense

of the world is really common madness. For

secular, external power dissipates as one grows

old, grows weak, grows sick, and dies.

The warrior realizes we are all in the process of

dying. His "common sense" is to forgo what

cannot possibly last, focusing instead upon

what is eternal—the way of death—

the true underpinning of life.

INNER ENERGY

Does the warrior, then, not partake of the play of

    energy and power?

On the contrary, he does so to the extreme.

However, the power of the warrior comes

    from within. It is not outwardly manifest.

It cannot be grasped, exchanged, or rewarded.

The power the warrior masters is his, and his alone.

It is an inner strength that can never be taken

    away.

The energy resides within,

    and will accompany the warrior to his death.

FREE POWER

Amazingly, the energy that matters is open to all.

It is free for the taking.

It is not hidden and esoteric.

It cannot be obtained by force.

It is simply a mind-set.

Some refer to it as wisdom.

The holy guru atop a mountain.

The serene and happy peasant.

The sanguine, old man unaffected by surrounding
turmoil.

They tread an inner course which all can
follow.

They know that wisdom and tranquility are what really
matter.

They understand that one has only oneself.

LOCATING THE ENEMY

The "enemy" resides anywhere there is contention.

This is the abstract enemy. Whether real or imaginary—

physical, emotional, or spiritual.

The enemy is anything that drains rather than enhances.

Conquering an enemy may not necessarily mean physical

destruction. It merely means neutralizing his power

over you.

To "conquer" is to overcome the effects on one's

internal balance.

LIFE AS A CHALLENGE

The warrior faces life as a continual challenge—

    a reveille for the spirit.

Each predicament is welcomed as a worthy opponent.

Every difficulty is just another test of his composure.

The warrior allows nothing to undercut morale.

    If hardships are allotted,

        it is merely a test of endurance.

    If things go wrong,

        it is a chance to make them right.

Complaints and whining are the province of losers.

A winner strives to change things,

    or merely accepts them for what they're worth.

ENDURANCE

Though the battle may become difficult,

    the warrior never complains.

It is the life he has chosen.

It is the way leading to death.

How silly to whine about hardship and pain.

    For suffering is implicit in his path.

Death has been freely chosen—

    not the comfort and security of life.

For this reason, the warrior suffers with dignity.

    Neither pain, nor isolation, can undermine

    his resolve.

NO COMPLAINTS

The true warrior has no complaints.

Whimpering and blaming he leaves to those of lesser skill.

For he realizes the drain of energy such

   negativity entails.

Why bother complaining when the same

   effort can make things right?

Why blame others instead of improving

   oneself?

The true warrior remains silent,

   and manifests his power throughout.

STRIVE

Knowing that life is war, how can one not only

survive, but win?

Realize that everyone fights for himself.

Commit all resources to winning your personal battle.

Enhance one's awareness, energy, and skill.

Mobilize one's forces.

Be ready at all times.

Expect nothing,

but be prepared for everything.

GOAL - ORIENTED

All warriors have goals although they may remain unknown.

The warrior is highly motivated although he seems totally

at peace—for he is content with what he has already

achieved.

And yet, he still wants more—

he wants perfection.

He wants to attain everything he can possibly achieve.

For he knows life is short and Death eagerly awaits.

The warrior strives constantly to improve, and to conquer

his limitations.

He realizes life is a challenge that must be met with a

call-to-arms.

For Death is ever-ready to seal one's fate.

AIM HIGH

When shooting at an elevated position, a good

archer aims higher than the target.

When shooting at a distant point he purposely

aims farther.

The natural force that pulls downward requires

this compensation in sighting.

In the same manner, a warrior aims higher and

farther in attempting his goal.

For even should he falter, he will gain

more than those who aim low.

He knows that those who attempt little,

often come up short anyway.

And if one should miss one's target,

it may as well be the stars.

THE UNCHALLENGED

What is even worse than aiming low, are those who fail
      taking aim at all.

Fear of failure and criticism keeps them from even picking
      up the bow.

They're unsure of what to aim at—
      and what if they should miss?

Their shortsightedness leads to paralysis of the bow-arm.

Their paralysis leads to excess energy of the mouth.

For it is easier to criticize the aim of others than to work
      and strengthen one's own arm.

Those who do—
      speak very little.

And those who speak—
      don't do much.

BRAVERY

The most courageous warrior is often the first to fall.

Those leading the charge take the brunt of the attack.

Risking oneself beyond the call of duty,

      projecting oneself into harm's way,

            are the signs of a true warrior.

Heroism and bravery come naturally because they

      are his avowed way of life.

No self-respecting warrior will cringe and timidly

      hold back.

For to show fear means that one is not on

      good terms with Death.

It is an admission that one is still merely a man.

The warrior spirit is immortal,

not because the warrior can't die,

but simply because death is no longer

a concern.

ALLIANCE

Knowing life is war does not mean everyone is an

      enemy. Alliances must be formed and cooperation

           sought for the mutual good.

Alliances, however, are often temporary. They are

      often broken on a whim. They should be seen

           for what they are: cooperation between two

           separate and disparate entities.

When all is said and done one ultimately fights one's

      own battle.

A DEADLY COMPANION

Because each warrior fights his own battle,

    he dies ultimately alone.

    Even his enemy leaves the field to avoid the

        sight of death.

    But Death has never left,

        remaining constantly at the warrior's side.

    In the end he is the warrior's only true companion—

        ever-faithful and eager to accompany him

        into the beyond . . .

COMPANIONS

When an enemy arrow is loosed, a false comrade

will duck and let you take the hit.

A true comrade will shout to take cover,

and hope you're quick to react.

A true friend will push you away,

and very likely get hit.

The warrior reads these signs of character and

responds accordingly.

He distances himself from false comrades,

walks beside true comrades,

and embraces true friends.

Needless to say, a warrior's life is very lonely.

ON ONE'S OWN

Though a warrior may rely, to some extent, on another—

      in the final analysis he must rely solely upon himself.

For the struggle of our life is our's alone.

Though others may appear on our side,

      they may easily turn tail and run.

They may change sides on a whim.

They may be enticed into slipping a knife in our back.

For this reason, the experienced warrior embraces comrades

      with a wary eye.

While gregarious and accepting, he nevertheless

      maintains a calm watch over his shoulder.

For the most devastating treachery is committed

      by our "friends."

TRUST

When rations are scarce, and when presented with

uneven portions, those who take the larger

portion can never be trusted.

Those who take the smaller portion are thoughtful

and polite.

Those who say they are not hungry can be trusted

with one's life.

Being dead already, the warrior has conquered hunger.

Shortage of food is simply another challenge—

no greater than fighting boldly in battle—

no worse than suffering a wound to the belly.

LOYALTY

When the battle is being lost, those who wander off

  seeking easier victories can never be trusted.

Those who stand by one's side are genuine comrades.

Those who rally one's spirit, and lead the charge,

  can be trusted with your life.

When the battle is being won, those who come to assist

  in your victory are to be doubted (where were they

   when you needed them?).

Those who were with you all the way deserve every

  merit and praise.

Those who wander off to help others, or merely

  slip into anonymity, deserve the greatest respect and

  and loyalty. They helped, not because of promises

  or possible rewards, but simply because your battle

was right, and now that you have won . . .

The true warrior chooses his battle because he believes

it is right,

and not because of prestige or profit.

DOING WHAT IS RIGHT

The true warrior follows the path of what is right.

This differs markedly from the path of righteousness.

The path of righteousness is a judgmental path that

endeavors to correct others.

Whereas the warrior strives only to correct himself.

Amidst chaos and confusion the path becomes clear.

Weighing the situation, balancing the pros and cons,

the warrior follows a course of action that he believes

is just.

The greatest warrior does what is right,

regardless of the consequences,

despite the harm that may befall him,

risking the censure or enmity of his
peers.

GENEROSITY

Humanity is divided by two distinct personalities:
  those who give, and those who take—
  those who are generous, and those who are selfish--
  those who are thoughtful, and those who are
  inconsiderate.

These opposite personalities have the natural tendency
  to attract.
Like a void that must be filled,
  abundance overflows into the abyss.

The warrior recognizes these traits and employs them to
  his advantage.

He can break the natural cycle and channel it to his own ends.
  Two voids can be pitted against one another until one or
  both are destroyed.
  Two abundances can be joined to create an empire.

The same practice can be applied in daily life.
  One's friends should be real friends,
    and not hidden parasites.
  One's enemies or competitors can fight each other,
    and not oneself.
  One can form an alliance or marriage which will
    empower, rather than detract.

The discerning warrior need only look into the "heart"

of the matter.

POSSESSIONS

The warrior pares down his possessions for freedom

and mobility.

He gives whatever he cannot take (and very little

can be taken where every warrior must go).

While this may appear as generosity, there is another

agenda involved.

Because the warrior lingers on the brink of death,

he is less concerned about material things.

What another man treasures, he considers an

immense burden.

By freeing himself of possessions, the warrior not

only creates good will and good karma,

but also lightens his sojourn into the beyond.

PASSING THROUGH

The stealthiest fighter is sleek and unencumbered.

Like a fast ship he is streamlined as he cuts his way

through life.

The less entanglements, the better.

The less baggage, the easier the passage.

The warrior never allows himself to be weighed down

and anchored. For he knows the barnacles will

take root, and his hull will rot.

THE TRAVELER

The warrior is a vagabond through life.

His heart finds no solace.

His feet find no rest.

Where the commoner labors to secure his place

in the world, the warrior knows the world

has no place for him to reside.

The warrior is restless and uncomfortable,

for there is nowhere he belongs.

For this reason his soul is always on the move.

It never grows complacent.

It is reluctant to settle down.

Rather than fortifying a permanent stronghold,

it is continually breaking camp.

For with Death constantly at his heels, the warrior

confronts, each moment, the transience of life.

HOMELESS

The true warrior belongs nowhere.
    He has no physical abode.

Although surrounded by friends and family,
    he is always alone.

Through fake smiles and curt greetings
    he remains distant and reserved.

His heart is never present.
    He never really feels at home.

For he is a soldier who may suddenly be ordered
    to the front.

Death is his commander who may revoke his leave
    without notice.

At any moment he may be forced to abandon everything
    and everyone.

And protocol demands no one witness his death-march
    into the beyond.

Whether for himself, or for others, "compassion"
    explains the warrior's coldness of heart.

INDIFFERENCE

Because the warrior is already dead, he greets life with

aloofness.

What matters most to the living he shrugs off with

indifference.

What do the dead care about accumulating wealth or

position?

What difference does it make what other people think?

Prestige, fame, accolades of the highest order . . .

An entire kingdom cannot be carried through the

narrow passage of death.

PRIORITY

The warrior knows what is important and what is trivial.

His ire cannot be goaded by miniscule events.

He cannot be taunted or teased into an inappropriate response.

For the warrior sees life more objectively than mere mortals.

Being dead, he realizes how much energy is wasted on the inane.

But this does not mean he cannot be angered.

It means he judges what truly deserves anger.

Discrimination must be impeccable.

For the warrior spirit, once aroused, will engulf

everything in its wake.

LIFE CREATES A WAKE

As the first action issues forth, there can no longer be peace.

Once moved, the world is no longer the same.

Here enters the warrior.

The warrior's realm is one of action.

It is also one of inaction.

The warrior's aim is to resolve conflict.

Ending strife regains balance and returns peace.

In effect, the warrior's task is impossible.

His actions, performed with diligence and

integrity, will stop the world.

SOLITUDE

Because all life is contention,

      because engagement of any kind is a form of battle,

           the warrior's tendency is to avoid conflict.

Avoiding conflict often means withdrawing from the arena.

Whenever possible the warrior seeks the peace of solitude.

Taken to extremes, the warrior keeps to himself.

Old age often finds him withdrawn and alone.

Legends tell of mountain-priests: the warrior-sage

      who seeks refuge and solace in the wilderness.

      Wisdom and power garnered from nature

      and nourished from within.

INTENTION

The results of an action fade with time.

Whereas the reason and decision to act

    remain forever.

The outcome of the battle is insignificant

    compared to the courage and struggle

      of the fight.

The way of the warrior is the way,

    and not the war.

The meaning of life is the meaning,

    and not the outcome,

      which is always death.

The shape and intention of his soul is how

    the warrior is ultimately defined.

DIGNITY

Regardless of circumstance, a warrior with

composure will never lose his soul.

Even Death itself cannot claim him completely.

On the other hand, should a warrior lose control

all becomes lost.

For even should he survive, what good would

it do?

Without his dignity, his soul, a warrior is

better off dead.

INDEFENSIBLE

Those who prey upon others,

    must themselves become prey.

Those who harm others,

    must in turn be harmed.

Such is the law of karma,

    the way of yin and yang, of cause and effect.

Because the warrior has no self,

    he cannot be preyed upon or harmed.

Because he dwells at the heart of nothingness—

    his emptiness is serene.

Because he is not of this world,

    he can no longer be reached.

Because he is nothing—

    there is nothing to defend.

CONSERVATION OF ENERGY

To be powerful, and yet restrained
      is the ultimate martial art.

To be tempted, and yet maintain control,
      is the highest form of self-discipline.

To be strong is to have the option.
One can do battle and disrupt the equilibrium—
      engaging the yin/yang—
      forcing karma into action.
Or one can hold back, find the neutral ground—
      allow face to be saved.

The superior warrior has nothing to prove,
      and thus avoids battle whenever possible.
He realizes that the highest martial art is
      non-contention—an arena where neither
      side loses, and yet both sides win.

By not turning the wheel of karma,
      by not disrupting the yin/yang—
      universal balance is preserved
      and energy is conserved.

PASSIVITY

The "nothingness" of life embraces much of oriental
   philosophy. It manifests in the oriental character
   trait of passivity.

What is calm and passive remains enigmatic, inscrutable.

What is turbulent and aggressive is more easily "read."

What is active can be studied until effective strategies
   are formulated.

What is inactive can only be guessed at——its unknown
   nature only surmised.

What is passive can thus restrain its forces while
   studying its opponent——like a hunter stalking
      his prey, like a master pondering his game plan.
   Only when certain of victory will his forces be
   unleashed.

The best strategy for an active force is to poke and
   prod the inactive into a response.
Hopefully it can strike and conquer before its
   own weakness is perceived.

THE WAY OF NO WAY

The ultimate martial art is one of non-contention. The warrior strives for perfection, but his highest aim is to be so proficient that he never needs to fight. Whether his reputation precedes him and frightens off opponents; whether he must periodically demonstrate his prowess; or whether, in combat, his bearing and attitude makes others shrink and withdraw—he is recognized as a force not to be contended with, a foe one doesn't wish to engage. This is the supreme level a warrior strives to achieve.

But, in the final analysis, what does this mean? That after a lifetime of hard work and diligent practice, of honing one's skill and ability—one has no opportunity to use them?

Rather than disappointment, the true warrior finds this a state of grace. For he realizes that the way of his art is ultimately the way of "no way"—the nothingness and emptiness at the heart of perfection.

WARRIORS OF PEACE

A warrior prepares all lifelong to engage in battle.

And yet there is never a battle.

The world is at peace.

Is this a tragic waste of a life, of one's energy?

NO!

For the true warrior, life itself is the war.

Every day he partakes of the battle.

The Way itself has become the real path.

The ultimate goal of all true warriors is not war.

"NO WAY" IS "THE WAY"

The great warrior understands that the true way is no way.

Life is contention—disruption—the yin and the yang eternally

in conflict, striving for balance.

Yet at the heart there is peace.

The true warrior is serene. He is at one with nothingness.

He understands the paradox of life—

and the paradox of his art.

And he is unperturbed.

He is the calm center about which all things revolve.

THE GREAT UNKNOWN

Legend has it that the greatest swordsman of all never fought in

any battles, not once engaged in a duel, never shed a drop

of blood.

Fellow practitioners were awed by his swiftness and agility, his

power and cunning. In mock-combat they attested to his

superiority—never being where they struck,

always striking them unawares.

Such was his prowess that no swordsman dared to challenge.

Rivals spying from afar soon grew faint of heart and withdrew.

Unlike other masters, whose fame grew upon the graves of their

challengers, this virtually unknown swordsman never had

any challengers, and so never grew famous. But

to masters he is regarded as the greatest swordsman of all

times simply by virtue of those he never had to kill,

simply because he had no need for fame.

THE NON - BATTLE

In the end the best fighting is no fighting.

And the most glorious battle is the one that

was never fought.

The greatest warrior returns with no mark,

and with no blood.

Without lifting his sword he retires undefeated.

PART TWO

MEDITATIONS

"What good are ideals

without a center

from which to manifest?"

CENTER

A spinning top is a whirlwind of energy,

    yet its central axis remains still.

A tornado wreaks havoc,

    yet the vortex of the funnel remains calm.

Calmness and stillness should thus be the

    center from which all action emanates.

BALANCE

A spinning top is graceful

    because it is a balance of force.

Bumps or wobbles will knock the

    whirling vortex wildly askew.

Balance is hence necessary for

    maximum efficiency.

Thus the warrior, epitomizing the

    essence of kung-fu, maintains a central

    point of balance throughout

    the whirlwind of his life.

SERENITY

The eye of a hurricane is calm while its

     arms lay waste.

The center is imperturbable while the

     periphery is chaotic.

The interior remains inviolable. It

     cannot be approached.

STILLNESS

The mind and heart must be still in order to

observe one's surroundings—

like the surface of a pond that clearly

reflects the moon.

Agitation creates wakes of ripples and

confusion.

Stillness creates a deep, perfect mirror.

Quiet and calmness are thus prerequisites for

a lightning response.

LISTENING TO ONESELF

Since the dead don't talk,

    neither should the warrior.

He refrains from the endless chatter that

    signifies the living.

He needs to express nothing

    because there is nothing to express.

His realm is one of isolation and permafrost.

It is remote from daily life.

If he speaks, a cold chill lingers in the air.

The surest way to generate internal energy is to

    simply remain silent. Rather than dissipating

    energy on idle chatter, the warrior communes

    internally with his own soul. His best friend

    is his inner self, for it is sympathetic, and yet

critical—genuinely concerned with his welfare

and development.

The patient warrior sits in silence,

but with ears cocked at the ready.

For only when quiet can the true self emerge.

SILENT ENERGY

A stone doesn't talk,
        neither does a mountain or glacier.

Instead, they remain silent,
        simply biding their time—
        for their realm is the eternal.

The glacier, by its mere presence, grinds
        mountains into dust.

The mountains buckle and grow into
        colossal backbones over time.

Like a mountain or glacier, the warrior
        sees himself as an implacable force
        of nature.

He is invincible, for nothing can stand
        in his way.

He keeps to himself until he is good
        and ready.

When primed for action, the volcano abruptly
        erupts.

The avalanche suddenly sweeps down.

Nothing can resist the relentless onslaught
of nature.

The only hope is to run or get out of the way.

A NATURAL FORCE

A volcano that erupts cannot be contained.

An earthquake that sends one tumbling cannot be stilled.

A hurricane must be allowed to vent its fury.

A tidal wave floods everything in its wake.

A bolt of lightning strikes without warning.

An avalanche sweeps down, consuming an

      entire village.

Having left humanity behind, the warrior must

      be contended with as a force of nature.

Inhuman, long since dead, he engulfs with

      total resolve.

Once triggered, he cannot be stopped until

      his energy dissipates, and his spirit comes

      to a natural rest.

HIDDEN POWER

That which is known must always be displayed
    and matched.

Those who are recognized and acknowledged are
    also constantly challenged.

One must practice as hard as one can merely to
    keep up, to keep fit.
It's all one can do simply to stay in the
    same place. One is always proving oneself
    to others—and to oneself.

On the other hand, hidden power is never challenged,
    but is always there.

Rather than being wasted on self-conscious displays,
    it is conserved and nurtured—allowed to grow
    into a dynamo of energy.

This latent power lies calmly just beneath the surface.
It remains dormant and unknown until it is forced
    to erupt.

The strategy is obvious: one is prepared for what is
    perceived as powerful.
One is unguarded for what is seemingly no threat.
The fortress is besieged by legions.
Whereas the hidden man-trap takes one unawares.

UNPREDICTABLE

That which is predictable is easily overcome.

Timing and positioning will create an effective
ambush.

For this reason, the warrior endeavors to remain
unknown.

He covers his tracks and manifests unexpectedly.

He keeps his true motives hidden while
broadcasting false intents and desires.

In this way, his real nature is never perceived nor
understood. His enemies are kept in disarray
and second-guessing. Even his friends have
no idea where he sleeps or what he dreams.

HIDDEN AGENDA

The best strategist keeps his objective secret.

For an adversary to know one's goal means probable
        defeat—he need only wait in ambush along the path.

Secrecy and misdirection are thus vital to the warrior.

He keeps his aims to himself so that his opponent is
        always wondering and worrying.

He works this way and that to lead his pursuers astray.

In this way, the warrior moves deftly through hostile
        terrain.

No one knows where he's going,
        or what is truly his aim.

SECRECY

Only a fool grabs an expert at grappling.

Only an idiot challenges an expert swordsman
      to a duel.

If one's strengths are known they lose efficacy
      and surprise.

The grappler will be beaten by fast kicks and strikes.

The swordsman will be defeated by a poisonous dart.

For this reason, all true warriors strive to conceal
      their abilities. Their strength must be their
      weakness—their weakness their strength.
Thus the trap is set for those willing to engage
      the unknown.

PERFORMING WITHIN

If constrained from practicing openly, one can always

practice secretly. If physical movements are

prohibited, one can still move within the mind.

Whether shackled in a prison cell; bound and gagged

as a wild man; incapacitated from injury or illness;

or simply traveling on a long journey—the mind

and spirit can be liberated despite physical restraint.

Set the chi flowing by performing movements and

exercises in the mind. Imagination will stimulate

chi centers and enhance vitality. Mental clarity and

sharpness will also accrue.

PRACTICE SECRETLY

The best practice is done without spectators—

    no one to judge, no one to impress, no one's

    favor or approval to gain.

Simply yourself—for yourself.

In a similar manner, to practice and then to speak

    of your practice, also diminishes its effect.

Even to inform others of your dedication

    depletes half its worth—because you are

    doing half of it for them.

The most powerful form of practice is thus hidden

    and unspoken. One's suffering and ecstasy

    reserved for oneself—alone.

EMPOWERMENT

Practicing before an audience, demonstrating one's

    prowess and skills, is the surest way to deplete

    resources and drain chi.

Contrariwise, practicing alone in the desert, honing

    one's abilities before no witness, is the surest

    way to conserve and enhance chi.

Therefore, the greatest warrior keeps silent about

    his practice, lets no one witness his skill,

    performs deep within the forest. For he knows

    that one word, one pair of eyes, may distract

    his spirit and become his undoing.

The tree falls within the forest making no sound—

    yet it falls.

ACTIONS - NOT WORDS

The best warrior speaks little,

> but accomplishes much.

Rather than talk,

> he prefers to act.

Where others make speeches about all the things

> they will do, the warrior (off to the side)

> does them many times over.

Much is lost in making pronouncements.

Once something is expected or promised,

> it becomes harder to do.

For energy is drained in vain, colorful flourishes.

The delightful task now becomes a dreaded chore.

A modest reserve often accompanies those who

accomplish great things—

not necessarily for virtuous reasons,

but merely because it requires less energy.

CHOOSING THE MOMENT

The warrior believes that he shapes his own destiny,

that he alone is responsible for every moment

of his life.

Thus he is never a victim.

He chooses the time and place of engagement.

Even when surprised,

the time is suddenly—NOW!

AFIRE

When fighting—fight.

When at peace—be peaceful.

Strive always for peace, but be prepared for war.
Refrain until there is no alternative but to
       fight—then fight wholeheartedly with no
       thought of peace.

Those initiating a fight have no desire for peace.
Those desiring a fight will often win.
For these reasons, when forced to fight, the
       peaceful man must also desire to fight.
Reluctance, timidity, and second thoughts
       will lose the day.

The peaceful man abhors violence, avoids causing pain.
The violent man enjoys hurting others, seeks out
       excuses to become vicious.
When combat begins—who will win?
To ensure victory the peaceful man must also
       become violent. Fight fire with fire. Otherwise
       the "nice guy" will certainly finish last.

MEETING RAGE WITH RAGE

When engaging an enraged opponent one must also

become enraged.

Controlled rage is necessary to counter the blinding,

overwhelming rage of a maniac.

Controlled rage pumps chi and aggression through the blood.

Its absence poisons chi with timidity and fear.

Fighting violence with increasing violence. The way to win is to

be even more murderous than your foe.

ANGER

Followers of the way have a saying that anger blinds.
This is true, but only to some extent.

Another saying is that the greatest warrior remains
        deadly calm—his anger cannot be roused.
This is also true—but again—only to some extent.

On the lowest level, anger causes tunnel vision—
        one can easily lose control, surrender judgment,
        forfeit awareness.
In this case, anger can be a detriment.

On another level, lack of anger can make one hold back,
        not follow through on a strike, show mercy—
        only to turn and be stabbed in the back.
Lack of anger can backfire with loss of spirit and vitality.
One lacks enthusiasm and is seen to be soft.
Lack of anger can make one lose the "killer instinct,"
        the "edge."

For most warriors, controlled anger is necessary to
        muster courage and strength. Without it they would
        be "pudding" to be molded to the enemy's will.

It is only on the highest, most enlightened level, that
        the warrior can safely do away with anger.
Only the supreme warrior, who masters everything,
        finds anger a blinding hindrance.

CONTROLLED ANGER

Anger is the warrior's greatest nemesis.
It is also his greatest friend.

When blinded to the point of fury, anger often
        causes a warrior's defeat.
He becomes heedless and irrational.
He loses his center and balance.

On the other hand, anger can lend a powerful
        jolt of energy, giving the warrior seemingly
        superhuman strength.
He loses his fear, and becomes bold
        and daring.
His rage can make him temporarily
        insensitive to pain.

Anger is thus a double-edged sword.
It can cut one's enemy.
Or it can cut oneself.

The true warrior knows how to control and use
        anger for his own purposes—
        rather than allowing anger to
        control and abuse himself.

UNMOVED

A person with heart inflicts pain

and is himself pained—

inflicts suffering

and himself suffers—

begins to destroy, hesitates,

and is himself destroyed.

A warrior must gain distance,

must by necessity become heartless.

Among the rank and file,

the nice warrior dies young.

COMMITMENT

If you must fight—then fight!

If you must run—then run!

Whatever action taken must be taken fully.

Whatever direction taken must be taken to the extreme.

To be a master one must know which way to turn.

ALL THE WAY

If you wish to kill—

    kill all the way.

If you wish to injure—

    injure fully.

If you wish to disarm—

    render harmless.

When invisible—

    blend in.

When provoking—

    stand out.

Every action or inaction must be total.

Because the natural tendency is to hold back—

    the warrior's maxim, "everything and more,"

        removes that lingering, vestigial restraint.

DETERMINATION

If you want something done—do it!

Desires and wishes are valid only if one <u>intends</u>

    to see them fulfilled.

Half-attempts, procrastination, lack of

    commitment waste time and energy.

The true warrior maintains total resolve.

RESOLVE

Total resolve is the deadliest weapon in the

warrior's arsenal.

Holding back is the surest way to defeat.

Simple resolve can sometimes triumph over finesse

or strategy.

Whereas the greatest plan can falter because of

a single doubt.

Of all military virtues, the warrior treasures

resolve above all.

For knowing that one <u>will</u> act is more important

than knowing how, when, or why.

THE CLEAN CUT

Virtue resides in the execution of the clean cut.

Intention.

Power.

Swiftness.

No remorse. No hesitation. No second thoughts.

No pity. A mind pure and empty in the movement.

The blade cuts cleanly through all self-doubt.

TAKING THE PLUNGE

At a certain stage in the battle-plan the warrior must act.

No more waiting for further reconnaissance.

No more jostling for position.

Planning, and then replanning, and procrastinating are endless.

A moment is reached when the warrior must leap.

The bow can only be stretched so long.

The arrow must be allowed to fly.

RESPONSE

The true warrior does not react, but rather responds.

To respond is to reflect before moving or taking action.

To react is a reflex which can be manipulated by the enemy.

By responding, one's actions are never fully predictable.

By reacting, one can be tricked and lured into a trap.

Too much reflecting before responding may also lead to

    one's downfall.

One may hesitate or procrastinate.

One may think oneself into a vicious cycle.

Action may come too late—if at all.

For this reason the warrior must tread the fine line between

    reflecting and reacting—

        knowing the ease which an excess of either can

        bring about one's demise.

ALERTNESS

If given warning that an attack is imminent one

naturally goes on guard. One is alert and

ready for battle.

Should the expected attack fail to materialize,

one relaxes, drops one's guard.

This is the time decisive victories are won. As

the guard drops, the thief enters unnoticed.

For this reason great warriors never drop their

guard. They are always alert, never taken

by surprise.

OVERBEARING

Those who place themselves upon a pedestal are asking

    to be toppled.

Those who swagger and boast merely invite envy and

    ill will.

Challenges are being issued to all within hearing.

It is only a matter of time before the "great"

    must fall.

For this reason, the true warrior strives to remain obscure.

Being hidden, his power is even more devastating

    when unleashed.

He wastes no time or energy fending off claims to

    his fame.

He endures because his power can be nurtured,

    and thus grows to fruition.

ATTENTION

It is better to practice one movement with full

attention than to practice a thousand while

half-asleep.

Movements for their own sake are merely exercise.

It is the mind and spirit that must develop

coordination with the body, for they guide

and govern the flow of chi.

All the physical practice in the world is nothing

if the mind and spirit are absent.

All the energy expended is merely a waste.

Focusing one move with full attention and intention

will generate chi and create the deadliest blow.

PRACTICING WITHOUT BEING THERE

The ultimate downfall of a warrior's practice is

not having presence of mind.

Too often one's spirit is distracted, or one is

physically or mentally tired.

In such a case practice becomes merely physical

exercise, doing nothing to develop spirit and

the flow of chi.

Better to practice a form once with full intention

than twenty times while in a daze.

A PAI IS A SONG

The secret to performing pai is to realize that
        each form is alive. They have a life of their
        own—a pulse, a flow of energy.
Too often forms are performed rigidly—
        a result of years of regimented drilling—
        monotonous and executed on command.
This is not the way of pai.

Pai must flow from move to move, blending into
        one continuous movement. Each move is like
        a note in a song—some are long and sustained.
Others are short and abrupt. Some build to a
        high climax. Others fade into silence.

Pai are physical music. They have a tempo and
        rhythm. The flow is dynamic, not rigid and
        static. There are ups and downs. There is
        excitement and there is peace.

Once the tune has been discerned, the form can
        be practiced, played upon, and eventually
        mastered. But the music must first be heard,
        otherwise it is all just empty wind.

SMUGNESS

The overly-praised often become satisfied with
      their achievement.

The conquering army often becomes drunk on the
      spoils of war.

The "champion" becomes overconfident, finding
      it unnecessary to develop and improve.

Smugness is thus the greatest enemy of the warrior.
It induces laziness and contentment, a false
      sense of security which precedes the inevitable
      downfall.

The famous become "has-beens" who live and die
      in the past.

The victors are despised and slaughtered as they
      sleep.

The "expert" is unexpectedly defeated by a rank
      amateur.

Thus the true warrior never falls prey to complacency.
He remains ever-vigilant, constantly striving to
      excel.

ARROGANCE

Those who know everything
      have nothing to learn.

Those who are complacent
      have nothing to do.

If hunger and thirst are sated,
      one is jaded by a full table.

If feet are bound and confined,
      they have no room to grow.

Therefore, the warrior strives to keep
      an open mind.

He greets life with an open heart.

Because his cup is empty
      it can always be filled.

Because he projects childlike wonder,
      he will constantly grow.

Those wishing to know must be willing
    to learn,
        because those who "know" will
          never learn.

The strongest warrior takes lessons
    from everyone,
        even from the enemy.

ALWAYS A BEGINNER

Regardless of skill and achievement the true warrior
    always considers himself a beginner. For in
    the vastness of the universe there is always
    more to learn.

Regardless of rank or level, the true warrior remains
    open to a new approach. For in this way he will
    never be taken by surprise.

Rigidity and closed-mindedness are the hallmarks of
    old age and weakness.
Flexibility and openness are the hallmarks of youth
    and energy.

Therefore, the greatest warrior is adaptable to change.
    He learns from everyone and adjusts to every
    situation. In effect, he has the mental state of a
    perpetual beginner—a child. He never acquiesces
    to a pattern. He never succumbs to being the
    "know-it-all." Humility and curiosity are his
    constant companions.

MULTIPLE CAMPAIGNS

In the battlefield of life many campaigns are
        waged simultaneously.

One's fortress must be built and secured.

Troops must be entertained and paid.

Enemies must be outmaneuvered or countered.

One's surroundings must be continuously
        patrolled and defended.

One must send scouts and mount expeditions
        into unknown territory.

New resources must be developed or else face
        depletion.

One's talent and skill must be honed to perfection.

One must learn and practice constantly.

One must be one step ahead.

For this reason the greatest warrior lives in
        perpetual battle.

There is never an excuse for "nothing to do."

A CHALLENGE

The greatest warrior views the worst threat as

a challenge.

The most disastrous situation,

The most powerful and evil opponent,

The weakest aspects of himself—

These are all causes to rally one's intent,

to conquer oneself.

Unchallenged, the warrior grows dull and listless,

Challenged, he is alert and becomes sharp

and bright.

UNYIELDING

Never give up.

Never give in.

The warrior fights on to the end—

    and then beyond . . .

Each moment is a personal challenge,

    a relentless struggle.

For the warrior the greatest betrayal is betrayal

    of oneself—surrendering to weakness,

        apathy, and discouragement.

The worst defeat

    is to defeat yourself.

The toughest battle is won within.

ATTITUDE

The greatest warriors have a mind-set that will
    admit no defeat:

A commitment, a dedication, a positive
    "go-for-it" attitude.

No excuses. No hesitation. No wishy-washy
    wavering. No procrastination so that
        nothing ever gets done.

"Let's do it!" they say cheerfully.
    Not tomorrow—right now!

They expect the most from themselves
    and from those around them.

Their attitude, from the start,
    makes the task halfway complete.

Such warriors may not be invincible, but their comrades
    (as well as their enemies) believe them nearly to
        be so. And such confidence and high morale is a
        good jump-off toward victory.

TENACITY

The most valuable lesson of the warrior:

Never say die.

This attitude can be applied to all aspects

    of life: social, financial, spiritual, artistic.

The tenacity of a warrior perseveres till

    his last breath—never yielding, never

        surrendering, never admitting defeat.

A legendary master used to say, "Get knocked

    down seven times—get up eight!"

The true warrior knows no discouragement.

"Defeat" never enters his vocabulary.

For even the worst is merely a temporary

    setback.

FRIENDLY POISON

Misfortune and deprivation are not shunned by the warrior.

If he gambles and then loses—

    those are simply the risks.

Boldness and daring are his natural bywords.

In the game of life there must be both winners and losers.

But to a warrior, any losses are met as challenges

    to overcome.

Thus, every loss is merely seen as a difficult victory.

The warrior fatefully accepts hardships as a test of

    endurance and fortitude.

If the pain doesn't kill him, it only serves to make

    him stronger.

He assimilates every poison into his being,

    transforming them into his own deadly venom.

LOSING TO WIN

Every battle does not end in victory.

Only one person can win any given contest or race.

For most people, life consists of many losses and

failures.

Therefore the warrior learns to regroup, reinforce,

reassess, and redeploy his forces.

He learns from his mistakes—

then practices and tries harder.

The end result being an overall successful campaign.

STATE OF MIND

But what comprises success?

Success does not always mean winning.

Success can also mean failure—

     if it's with the right state of mind.

The greatest warrior reigns victorious—

     even when he happens to lose.

LEADERSHIP

Those who will not lead themselves,

    must wander aimlessly,

        or be led by others.

All true warriors are themselves leaders.

They can lead themselves.

They can lead others.

They can even be led—

    but only in their own direction.

If the way is dark,

    someone must light the path.

If the world is in chaos,

    someone must create order.

The true warrior starts within,

    and the within spreads—without . . .

FOLLOW THE LEADER

Those who wish to lead

must also know how to follow.

And they must know when to lead,

and when to follow.

WHAT IT TAKES

For a leader to emerge,

    he must separate from the crowd.

A sapling will be stunted by too much surrounding growth:

    hemmed in on all sides,

        nutrients sapped from its roots,

            light cut off from above.

To grow powerful,

    a warrior must stand on his own.

To live free,

    a <u>leader</u> must disentangle his roots.

Too much shelter,

    and not enough light will enter.

Unprotected, embraced by both wind and storm,
    roots are forced deeper—
    the foundation grows strong.

EACH HIS OWN GENERAL

Because everyone is his own general,

    everyone thinks he is in command.

In reality, one relinquishes command to

    many factors.

Knowing and overcoming these factors

    reestablishes control.

Understanding the weakness of others

    makes one a general to his army.

Understanding one's own weakness

    makes one a general to oneself.

DEDICATION

From one hundred students only one will become a master.

From one hundred masters only one will transcend.

Many attempt lofty goals,
        but few make it to the heights.

When faced with difficulties,
        most never even try.

Laziness and lack of drive take their toll.
Excuses are rampant.
Commitment and dedication fall to the wayside.

The true warrior, however, welcomes hard work and
        adversity. They are the tools with which he
            hones his skill, toughens his will, strengthens
        his soul.

The true warrior thus becomes as resilient as metal.
        His body becomes impervious to pain.
        His calluses shield him from evil intent.

LEADERLESS

Rely upon a leader,

      and the leader may be gone.

Rely upon yourself,

      and you are always there.

Each warrior must be a leader himself,

      paying deference only because it is his choice.

In this way, no matter how many heads are severed,

      the legendary dragon will grow ever more.

BEHEADING

As the arms and legs follow the orders of the mind,

    so does an army follow the commands of its leaders.

Sever the head,

    and the hands and feet become useless.

Concentrate on the <u>rea</u>l enemy,

    not on the peripheral.

SACRIFICE

Sometimes one must forfeit an arm in order to

remove a leg.

Sometimes one must forfeit a leg in order to

remove a head.

A troop can be lost if it will save a regiment.

A regiment can be lost if it will save an army.

Though painful, these exchanges are how wars

are won.

Sacrifices are made expediently to seize the

advantage.

THE BIG PICTURE

What separates a leader from the rank and file is

    his ability to see the larger perspective.

He distances himself from the blood and guts.

He rises above petty anger and vengeance.

Rather than taking a few easy victories,

    he pursues a far more costly advantage.

Rather than immediate retribution,

    he nurtures his anger for a strategic blow.

The greatest general views the battlefield from

    a cosmic level:

Each engagement being merely a small piece

    of the giant puzzle.

JUDGMENT

As a strategist, the warrior is quick to surmise.

He appraises the situation and offers

    summary judgment.

He is not shackled by wavering indecision and doubt.

Vacillation and fence-riding he leaves to

    the weak-minded.

Because he is quick to judge, the warrior is

    also quick to take offense.

He reads the nuances of a word or gesture.

In a flash, he understands the true intent.

A good leader and strategist quickly determines

    the rules of the game,

        the scope and the boundary,

            as well as just where each player stands.

TAKING OFFENSE

What others gloss over or forget,

  the warrior ponders and remembers.

What was the real intent of that comment?

Why the snickering or the funny look?

The warrior's code is one of honor that cannot

  be breached.

For a little hole here or there will lead to

  an unsound portage.

Eventually the hull will open and the ship

  will sink.

The warrior, being by nature a land animal,

  very rarely goes to sea.

SUSPICION

The greatest warrior is also the most guarded.

He is aware of all traps,

      realizes what is in front and what is behind,

         and takes nothing for granted.

Because of this wariness, he may appear unbalanced.

But it is merely a precaution that keeps him

      always on his toes, always one step ahead.

He is sensitive to the extreme.

And yet, while constantly vigilant and responsive,

      he nevertheless manifests calmness and serenity.

For only out of the void can an echo be heard.

RECRUITMENT VS. CONSCRIPTION

Discrimination is a requisite in building one's army.

Discernment must be shown in choosing worthy guards.

One's castle can be infiltrated because of one

    sleeping watchman.

One's fortress can collapse because of one weak

    support.

Scrupulousness is thus paramount in shaping one's

    forces.

Out of desperation one should never accept what

    just happens to be around.

FAITHFULNESS

Since life is an ongoing battle, discrimination must be
shown in the selection of comrades.

One cannot be everywhere at once. Someone must guard
one's backside.

Loyalty and trust are thus necessary with those close at hand—
the fatal mistake being the stab in the back.

What good is enlisting the greatest warriors if all are not
fighting on the same side?

For this reason talent and ability are only of secondary
importance.

Faithfulness and honesty are of primary concern.

Out of loyalty and friendship,

the mangiest dog in the pack

may be the only one who barks the alarm.

UNDERESTIMATION

Underestimating one's adversary makes one careless,

unguarded. One takes things for granted.

Holes are created in one's defense by one's own

sense of invulnerability. One's confidence

and cockiness are the most powerful weapon

in the enemy's arsenal.

For this reason the true warrior never underestimates.

He is always wary and on-guard.

He suspects every bum to be an agent in disguise.

Every drunkard he passes may be the national champion.

This cautious respect for all people keeps him ever on

his toes. Ironically, it also fosters a better relationship

with his fellow man.

DISGUISE

The greatest warrior is also a great actor.

He can play many roles—making others

      perceive an illusion.

By assuming any disguise, he can merge with

      and infiltrate the opposition.

He can gather intelligence or gain

      someone's confidence.

He can withdraw or strike in the dead of night.

The warrior-in-disguise is a wolf in sheep's clothing—

      biding his time in preparation for the kill.

MASKS

A crippled beggar takes one unawares as he suddenly
    charges at a full run.

A humble peasant can disarm everyone when he bursts
    forth as a skilled swordsman.

A charming courtesan can kill with impunity in the
    violent throes of passion.

A sentry in friendly uniform can easily stab one in
    the back.

The mask is thus a guise for catching one's opponent
    off-guard.
It is the means for gaining entry into the
    enemy stronghold.
It is also the means for escaping, unnoticed,
    in the crowd.

The true warrior is constantly masked to confuse
    those around him.
The danger is in acting so well that one
    confuses even oneself.

The mask that fools everyone can be difficult
    to remove.

CAMOUFLAGE AND MIMICRY

Insects and animals often survive by blending with

the landscape.

The weak remain unmolested by displaying the markings

of the strong or the distasteful.

Simply through trickery and skillful ruse many

disastrous encounters can be sidestepped.

The crafty warrior thus knows how to withdraw and

fade away.

He also knows when to display his colors, flaunt his

regalia, and beat his drums.

The most subtle warrior can often win without even

trying.

Without engaging in a single battle he

can move, unchallenged, to his goal.

AT PEACE

In times of peace the discerning warrior will become

peaceful, and thus indistinguishable from

the crowd. His calmness masks his natural

aggressive intent.

In times of war this clever warrior will also appear

at peace. The demeanor of a priest disconcerts

all potential attackers. When hearts are inflamed,

a dispassionate ease seems cold and calculating.

The boldest enemy is unnerved and will waver

in his resolve.

Thus, whether at war or at peace, the true warrior

remains calm and collected. For serenity is a

cloak that can never be undone.

A MAGICIAN

The greatest warrior is a magician who knows how
        to appear and disappear.
He also knows when.

One moment he exists,
        the next moment he is gone.

Was he only a figment?—
        a nightmare to contend with?
His startling display of war colors makes him
        all too real.
Yet his sudden vanishing makes him seem only
        fog and mist.

The true warrior appears only when needed.
He never lingers after-the-fact.
No one can accuse him of outstaying his welcome.
For in the blink of an eye,
        he is suddenly gone.

PROVOKING FEAR

In nature, mock battles often determine dominance.

The most fearsome gesture, the loudest bark,

the most vicious snarling and snapping, the

roughest play-fighting. Often battles are

avoided simply by inspiring fear, evoking awe,

making an impression.

The same is true of human beings.

Instilling fear in an opponent ensures his downfall.

Once frightened, the battle is already lost.

It is merely a matter of mopping-up.

The battle may not even be necessary. An inhuman

glance, a sudden menacing gesture, an aura

radiating that one should be left alone.

The first one frightened must back off or be consumed.

EXPERIENCE

If someone wants to be strong——let him tire until

    he becomes weak, then with a sudden burst

        of energy overtake him in the last stretch.

A whirlwind should not be met head-on. It must

    be sidestepped, avoided, and encircled.

Eventually it can be timed and entered.

Its force will be dissipated by its frenzy.

Youth and power should not be taken lightly.

But experience, knowledge, and maturity

    are, at the very least, a good match. And,

        if utilized well, will win the day.

AGING

With old age comes aching bones, weakening muscle-
  tone, lack of agility. One feels tired and stiff.
But these drawbacks can be accepted with grace
   and serenity. For with age can also come
     fearlessness and the awesome power of intent.

After a long, fulfilling life an aging master may be
  truly ready to die at any moment. Unlike a
  brash, young braggart who still harbors a lust
  for life, the master has the psychological edge
  of fearlessness. If he dies—so what. This
  secret of intent is more powerful than muscles
  or quick reflexes, for it empowers the master
  with boldness and the willingness to gamble
  it all.

Never underestimate or ridicule the frail, old warrior.
For doing so may indeed provide him the last
  laugh.

SUDDEN DISPATCH

Among warriors a story is told of a champion fighter
      defeated permanently is his last, unexpected bout.
He was young and powerful, a domineering brute
        who enjoyed intimidating others. After a few drinks
        at a tavern, the brash show-off ferreted out his next
        and last prey: a frail, old man in his seventies, a
        member of a different clan. The champion teased
        and taunted, ridiculing the lameness of the other
        clan. He badgered and insulted while thrusting and
        pushing with his massive chest. Then (unfortunately
        for him) he drew his sword to make the other beg
        for his life.
But suddenly the roles reversed. In a flash it was over.
        The decrepit, old man pulled a slim dagger
        from the sleeve of his robe, thrusting it deeply into
        the heart of the bully. It took only a split second. The
        matter was resolved with sudden dispatch. All witnesses
        told authorities the old man was simply defending his
        life.

A keen warrior takes nothing for granted.

What is seemingly harmless can easily conceal

      one's doom.

LOOKING BACKWARD

A common saying among ruthless warriors is "never look back."
This dictum refers to a necessary coldness after battle—
    after the carnage one should "have no regrets."

However, looking back has its advantages if one can learn from
    one's mistakes.
By reformulating strategies one can gain insight from
    hindsight.
No warrior ever became great who ignored his past.

And yet, being consumed by the past is also a grave danger.
One runs the constant risk of bumping headlong into
    the future.
A fine line must therefore be tread between looking
    forward and backward.

The best warrior is a scout who can see farther ahead than
    others, and yet casually glances back at the terrain
    he has just left.
Such warriors in life will never become lost.

CROSSROADS

At any crossroad, where the best path is unknown,

    the warrior must weigh the pros and cons. He

        may send out scouts, scour maps, peruse the

        logistics, but in the end he makes a choice.

Whether through intuition or reasoning he comes

    to a resolve. He does not waver or vacillate.

He sets out with determination along his chosen

    path.

This, however, does not mean he becomes blind to

    new evidence. He is always open to the possibility

        that he may very well have chosen wrong. If such

        is the case, he is the first to realize his mistake.

He is not averse to turning back. But he will do so without

reproach or complaint. He will do

so, as a warrior, with firm resolve and determination—

just as when he first started out. For, in fact, the

decision to return is regarded not as a mistake,

but as simply one more crossroad along his path.

RISK

Because life is constant warfare there is always

an element of risk.

While mastery of the traditional approach is

essential to the warrior, no new strategy

was ever developed by sticking securely

to the old.

The true warrior must have the boldness to act

upon a new vision. For responding unpredictably

is what makes him unique.

The greatest warriors are individuals who have

the strength and courage to dream.

BREAKING MOLDS

Molds must be broken in order for the warrior to grow.

As a butterfly bursts from its cocoon,
>   as a snake sloughs off dead skin,
>   as a deer drops its antlers—
>   so, too, must a warrior lose what is old.

For the forms that shape one's essence soon become
>   stultifying and restrictive.
The child must eventually rebel against the
>   suffocating influence of its parents.
The fledgling must leave the nest in order to fly.

The true warrior must also vanish in order to become
>   anonymous—in order to die.
For the old molds trap him in the past, whereas
Death (his destined mate) resides solely in the future.

The most unpredictable warrior continually breaks
>   molds and departs.
In this way he always grows, while always
>   remaining unknown.

The approach of a great warrior is signaled by loud
clamor and crashing.
And yet, when he appears, no one knows he is there.
>   For he is unrecognizable.
>   His form is never the same.

DEADLY EFFICIENCY

A famed swordsman became a legend for his innovative
draw. Instead of wearing his scabbard with blade
up, as is traditional, he drew his sword from a
scabbard with the blade facing down.

The traditional draw required the sword to move up,
overhead, and then either strike down or drop down
to an on-guard position.
Whereas the innovative draw fatally surprised many
opponents because it was the exact opposite of what
was expected. The sword was drawn from blade-
down to blade-forward, sweeping and slicing up the
front of the adversary. The simple draw had actually
become a surprise attack.

The famed swordsman was already one step ahead. His
opponents were sliced open before an attack of their
own was even possible. The innovation had fused
two distinct moves (the draw and the cut) into one
graceful, deadly, and surprising flow of energy.

ONE - UPMANSHIP

When life and death are in balance, one-upmanship

    is the rule.

If claws are extended—pull out a knife.

If a knife is drawn—pull out a sword.

If a sword is drawn—engage with a spear.

By remaining one step ahead, the warrior retains

    the upper hand.

By retaining control he will usually win.

FORESIGHT

The greatest warrior is always one step ahead.

Being one step ahead,

    he reigns victorious.

PART THREE

STRATEGIES

"What good are ideals and a center

without plans for implementation?"

PIVOTING

When turning to the left be aware of the right.

When turning to the right be aware of the left.

In this way balance and center are maintained.

YIELDING

If the right side is pressured, yield the right

    and extend the left.

If the left side is pressured, yield the left

    and extend the right.

If struck from above, duck down and cut the roots.

If struck from below, leap down from the clouds.

FAKING

Fake low, but strike high.

Fake high while striking low.

Fake to the left, but strike to the right.

Fake a retreat, but suddenly pivot and drop—

    striking back from a firm, low stance.

The attacker will literally run into your

    punch or kick, impale himself on your

      spear planted in the ground.

This tactic is known as "stretching

    him out."

POSTURE

If your opponent leans forward—draw him in

and down.

If he leans backward—press and topple him over.

Attach oneself to the heavens—always maintaining

balance and posture.

FIGHTING OFF - BEAT

A dancing fighter sets a rhythm.

Bobbing, weaving, shuffling feet.

Eventually the beat can be discerned.

Time the attack to the rhythm and strike offbeat.

PUNCHING THROUGH

When delivering an attack, see your fist or foot

    passing through your opponent. Full force

        of impact ends on the other side of his body.

Your opponent has simply "gotten in the way."

Visualize your punch not simply hitting his face,

    but striking the space just behind the back of

        his head. Your energy must not stop driving

        until that point is reached.

The warrior annihilates his enemy by seeing through

    him. His "intention" is beyond whatever stands

    in his way.

STRONG NEUTRALITY

To show passivity to an aggressor is to invite

an attack. To show weakness in the face

of strength is to allow domination.

To show aggression to an aggressor is to issue

a challenge. To show strength in the face

of strength is to invite struggle and competition.

The middle ground is the path of wisdom and

tact. To be neutral, and yet strong—

to stand straight and wobble neither backward

nor forward. To be fearless, and yet show

no provocation.

KNOW THE ENEMY

Knowledge and intuition are indispensable to the
       warrior. In confrontations, the first move may also be
       the last. Care should therefore be taken to instinctively
       size up the situation.

Opponents will behave differently according to their
       nature and conditioning. Even those who are similar will
       react varying upon their mood.

In the wild, animals must also be contended with
       according to their nature, as well as to the circumstances
       of the encounter.

Eye contact with many predators is reacted to as a
       challenge. Some are provoked to attack, while others may
       slink away in fright.

Raising arms, clothing, or baggage above one's head
       makes one appear larger and more intimidating to some.
They will shrink and disappear. Whereas others will take
       the gesture as a threatening display—a challenge to which
       they must respond.

Some animals will react to a loud, aggressive shout.
To others a calm, gentle voice works miracles.

Standing one's ground, stomping one's feet, or even
        charging may work with some. To others it may be better
        to back off and slowly retreat.

Mothers protecting their young are often vicious
        and maniacal.

Animals guarding their prey or territory can become
        formidable.

With humans, pride, obstinacy, and saving-face are
        determining factors.

If backed into a corner, even the most timid may have
        nothing to lose.

"To know one's enemy" is thus a requisite for victory.

Without knowledge and keen intuition, the slightest
        gesture, the wrong word, may provoke an undesirable
        fate.

The best general must be both a naturalist and
        psychologist. He understands how the enemy can be
        baited—what moves will force him to react.

ELIMINATING THE ENEMY

When pressed against the wall,
      the weakest opponent suddenly
      becomes formidable.

Having nothing to lose,
      he panics with a pent-up outburst
      of chi.

Thus, rather than cornering such a wild
      animal, surprise and subterfuge are the
      preferred methods of ensuring success.

1. Lull the enemy into a false sense of security,
      then overturn him while he rests.

2. Appear weak while secretly amassing your
      reserves.
3. Feign injury, then explode as he closes
      for the kill.

4. Strike when least expected.

5. Strike where least expected.

6. Strike cleanly with full intention.
      Cut the roots with one blow.

TACTICS

In the most heavily fortified wall

    there is always a crack.

The larger the army,

    the more traitors, cowards, and weaklings.

Use this vulnerability to overcome your enemy.

Use this warning to protect yourself.

ENERGY TRANSFER

Loose and limber—then hard and rigid.
Like a whip let loose—at the last moment cracks.
The power is generated from softness lashing out
      and suddenly becoming hard.

Hardness enters hard—the damage is purely physical
      and mechanical.

Softness entering and becoming hard causes internal
      disruption—the results are hidden and incalculable.

Therefore a backhand strike or slap, a roundhouse kick,
      or a two-fingered whip to the eyes should be loose
      and soft until the very last moment—merging with,
      covering or enveloping the target—then suddenly
      hard and rigid as iron while exploding from within.

The chi erupts out of the transfer of states. The damage
      inflicted generates from within. The strike is a
      transfer of internal energy—not a result of mere
      external force.

COILING

A compressed spring explodes when its tension is

released.

A tornado blasts to pieces anything in its path.

A whirlpool sucks in people and sometimes even

boats.

Thus, power resides in the momentum of a quick

spin, pivot, or twist.

Whether from the lash of a spinning back kick,

the penetration of a drilling punch, or the

twisting palm strike of the internal arts,

power is multiplied by coiling and then

snapping out.

SCOUTS

A large force has many eyes.

Birds feed and flock together because a
        predator has less chance to attack.
One eye will spot the intruder and
        sound a warning.

An army deploys scouts so as not to be
        surprised.

An individual must likewise deploy the
        scouts of his five senses.
Keep alert to any sound.
Inspect and interpret any sign.
Be aware of unusual smells.

With fine tuning and experience a sixth
        intuitive sense will be honed. When
           this happens the warrior can never
        be surprised.
Even while asleep he is ever vigilant.

COMPREHENSION

The broader the outlook,

    the greater the need for a plan.

The larger the terrain,

    the more necessary a map.

As the scope is enhanced.

    a general expands his horizon.

As the warrior becomes great,

    he encompasses the entire battle—

        from the first minor transgression

            to its ultimate repercussion.

He senses the cosmic implication of

    each and every act.

SURVEYING THE FIELD

A good leader scopes out the terrain before

    sending in troops:

Every obstacle, every hill and rock,

    every ditch and pond, every tree and

      ridge, every stand of grass.

The battlefield is the game of life.

The warrior assesses his chances.

He maneuvers mentally about the landscape,

    calculating the favorableness of each

      position.

When the game begins, he knows exactly where

    he wants to be.

He knows, in advance, which obstacles to avoid,

    and which must be overcome.

MISTAKES

If the western approach is difficult,

approach from the east.

If the lower gate is heavily guarded,

enter from above.

The warrior learns from his mistakes.

He abhors banging his head against a wall.

ADMITTING MISTAKES

The true warrior readily admits when he is wrong.

The reason: to amend his failings.

The need to "always be right," to "never admit a

    mistake," is an unwillingness to adapt—

        to think oneself perfect.

Rigidity and inflexibility can easily be pigeonholed,

    marked, and read. It will lead to your downfall.

What is stagnant eventually rots, like a quagmire

    stuck in its rut.

By admitting one's failings one can learn and grow,

    like a powerful stream overflowing obstacles,

        yet always ready to alter its course.

AVERTING FORCE

A powerful force should not be met directly.

Two rams that butt heads will both be sore.

The larger and stronger will always win.

It is pure mechanics.

Therefore, whether your force is strong and massive

> or small and weak, directly encountered force

> should be avoided. For even if one is larger,

> one will still be damaged to some degree.

Instead, step aside and deflect the opponent.

Or redirect by helping his energy to continue past.

Or strike out and allow his own momentum to

> double his pain.

PULLING IN

As the enemy presses forward,

    yield gradually to draw him in.

Then suddenly surround and smother him

    from all sides.

Isolate and cut him off from his source.

Then assimilate and absorb his wasted

    energy into your being.

MANIACAL FIGHTING

Tactics change rapidly when maniacal fighting is
        employed. The difference between traditional
        and maniacal fighting is as great as between
        the sun and the moon, between night and day.

Traditional fighting assumes an aura of guardedness
        and security. The health, welfare, and
        preservation of oneself and one's forces is
        integral in weighing the pros and cons of
        tactical engagement. The balance between
        damage inflicted upon an enemy and damage
        sustained plays heavily in shaping military
        strategy.

With maniacal fighting, however, these factors
        are of no concern. The maniacal fighter does
        not weigh gain against loss. All he cares
        about is loss—your loss. He doesn't care
        what happens to himself, so long as you are
        hurt as well. This single-mindedness makes
        him a truly fearless opponent, for fear is
        worrying about one's own well-being.

Taken to the extreme, the maniacal fighter is
        suicidal. He will kill you even if it means
        killing himself. He simply doesn't care.
He is guided by different rules.

ENGAGING A MANIAC

How to fight a suicidal maniac?
Avoid as far as possible. Keep the greatest
       distance. The suicidal fighter will take you
       down with him—even if you "win."

An example of a maniacal encounter:
Two opponents with equally-styled knives,
       equally well-trained, of equal weight and
       stature. One is a traditional fighter, the
       other is a maniac. The traditional fighter
       takes a stance, may dance about, make a few
       feints to feel out his opponent's ability.
He is evaluating and awaiting an opening.

What does the maniacal fighter do?
He doesn't care about waiting for an "opening."
He will create one inside of you.
He doesn't care about strategy or timing or stances.
All he cares about is killing you with his knife.
He doesn't care about your knife.
He doesn't care about his own life.
In one sudden lunge he throws himself at you
       with knife slashing, stabbing, and thrusting.
If you cut him—oh well.
It doesn't really matter.

SURVIVING A MANIAC

Run: it is the best defense.

However, this will probably frustrate and

    inflame his anger. If possible it will drive

        him even more berserk. But if you're the

            better runner . . .

If not . . .

His energy will be forward.

Evade: sidestep or duck and pull his momentum past.

Then strike from the side or from underneath.

Allow his own uncontrolled momentum to engineer

    his downfall.

DREAM - FIGHTING

In preparing for engagement, dreams are an ally

of the warrior. Scenarios can be anticipated;

fears and failings overcome.

When pursued or alarmed, the warrior should learn

to control his panic. The dream is believed

to be real and is therefore a valid training-

ground for waking life. Dream opponents

(monsters and maniacal murderers) are often

bigger and more powerful as imagined.

Therefore, mastering one's fears, confronting

and subduing a dream-foe, may make

subjugating "real-life" opponents a snap.

If nothing else, one will be desensitized and

calm, for after all, it's happened so many times before.

DREAMING THE SAME DREAM

A mind filled with thoughts and emotions is open
        to destruction. The warrior is distracted.
He is not present in the moment.

An attack breaks through causing surprise and alarm—
        as though awakening one from a dream—
        catching the warrior unprepared.

A good preparation is to dream of nothing:
keep the mind empty for a lightning response.

But the best preparation is to be dreaming the dream
        of the attacker so that one awakens anticipating
        battle. The warrior cannot be taken by surprise
        because he knows what is happening. He has
        already dreamt it.

It is said that the ability to dream the dream of one's
        opponent is rare. It is a skill that singles out
        the grandmaster.

(This tactic is known among peace-keepers as
        "identifying with the criminal"—getting into
        the mind of the murderer.)

FRIENDS AND ENEMIES

When surrounded by friends be open and honest.

When surrounded by enemies be closed and guarded.

Never make the mistake of treating your friends as

enemies or your enemies as friends.

Though it may seem obvious, the mistake is common.

It is often the reason for disappointment and an

early demise.

Knowing when to be open and honest or closed and

guarded is the beginning of wisdom.

MISTAKEN IDENTITY

Knowing that misplaced trust can lead to an early demise,
      the warrior takes advantage of this common mistake.
Though referred to as "dirty tricks" and the "sucker
          punch," the strategy is more respectably termed
          "practical street-fighting."
In other words, when life and death hang in the
      balance there are no rules. "Anything goes."
"Whatever works."

Whether one employs these tactics depends on the situation
      and one's ethics. But in any case one should be on
      guard for this strategy.

1. How to utilize mistaken identity?
Feign friendship—open arms—joviality—slap-on-the-back.
Enter your opponent's space in a disarming manner, close
      in with his guard down. Then, without warning, drop him
      and clean up.

2. How to guard against these practices?
Remain wary. Keep your distance. Back off (if necessary).
Never drop your guard. Being ready for a surprise, makes
      surprise impossible.

3. How to win at this point?
Go him one further. Pretend you've fallen for his
      dissembling. Pretend trust. Pretend to drop your
      guard. Then, when he closes in, surprise him instead.

"Traitor!" "Spy!" "Coward!" "Stabbed in the back."
These terms are considered dishonorable by many.
However, to many (<u>too</u> many) they are simply the tricks
of the trade.

ADVANTAGE OF BEING OUTNUMBERED

An arrow shot into a crowd will almost surely hit some mark.

No real accuracy is needed since the target is so large.

No time is consumed in aiming.

No energy is wasted since even a wild shot is rewarded.

A crowd cannot pursue through the hiding space of an individual.

When squeezing through a narrow crack a group of a
      thousand becomes only one.

Crowd mentality is limited and can easily be tricked.

"Follow-the-leader" and "no responsibility" rule group
      thought.

A member of a group feels less pressure to perform
      effectively. His shots are often wide of the mark.
After all, his shot is only one of a barrage.

He also feels less threatened. If he misses, and you
      then turn to shoot back, he is only one amidst a huge
      crowd. Whereas if he alone were in pursuit, he alone
      would be the target.

DISADVANTAGES OF BEING OUTNUMBERED

A hundred arrows launched at you will almost surely
    hit the mark—repeatedly. Therefore, concealment
    and strategic positioning are essential. Hit-and-run,
    fast escapes, disguise and blending-in are tactics
    required when outnumbered.

Even when "squeezing the cracks" the crowd has an
        advantage: it has a hundred heads. As the legendary
        monster each head severed sprouts another in its place.

And with a hundred heads comes two hundred arms.
Just as an octopus, the crowd has the singular advantage
        of branching out and encircling with its many arms. If
        deployed correctly escape may be nearly impossible.

Simply by virtue of size a crowd can instill fear. Before the
        first blow the pursued may have already given up.

The true warrior, therefore, battles each individual and
        does not fight the crowd as a whole.
Contrariwise, he also views the crowd as merely an
        individual (a big bully), and does not see himself
        overwhelmed by a teeming army.

ENTERING THE GATE

If your opponent is smaller, guard the lower gate

and collapse the heavens.

If your opponent is larger, guard the upper gate

and cut the roots.

Remember, a skilled warrior knows these principles.

Should this be the case then guard all gates

and attack the opposite, unnatural opening.

The greatest warrior is flexible and adapts to the

circumstance.

DISTRACTION

Distraction is an effective tactic for overcoming

    an opponent.

It is the easiest means of penetrating a defense.

The warrior must therefore guard against such diversions.

He must be ever aware—never fully engaged.

The true warrior's attention must be powerfully

    diffused like the sun—

    not concentrated like a candle illuminating

    only one's feet.

SLEIGHT OF HAND

If an opponent points <u>there</u>,

> a good warrior looks <u>here</u>.

If an opponent points <u>here</u>,

> a good warrior looks <u>there</u>.

Distraction is a key strategy for winning battles.

Awareness is the antidote for shortsighted stumbling

> into traps.

The greatest warrior looks everywhere,

> and yet, at the same time, nowhere.

He remains immune to minor distractions as he

> sets his own counter-trap.

TUNNEL VISION

When fearful or panicked, those afraid look straight ahead.

Their vision accommodates only the immediate threat.

Thus, they are vulnerable to attacks from above, below,

  behind, and from all sides.

This is the reason for the injunction to conquer one's fear

  and remain calm.

Peripheral vision will expand into the broader outlook.

Awareness will take in and encompass all around.

A master warrior, being fearless, thus cannot be surprised.

For he is serene and can sense any hostile intent.

SURPRISE

Of all fighting tactics the element of "surprise"

     is the most effective.

Nothing is worse than being hurt without warning.

Nothing is more disturbing than being caught unprepared.

"Surprise" demoralizes the most formidable opponent—

     makes him feel weak and vulnerable—

     makes him lose confidence and self-esteem.

"Surprise" undermines not only the leader,

     but the ranks.

It is the one element that can destroy the

     enemy from within.

THE UNEXPECTED

The hardest fall is the one that is unexpected.

The deadliest blow catches one by surprise.

The warrior is therefore prepared for a fall at

    any time. He is ready at every moment

    to avoid the unseen.

Conversely, the warrior practices the art of the

    unexpected.

    1. He employs stealth in his maneuvers.
    He is never seen nor heard.
    He appears when least expected.
    He disappears without a trace.
    He is never where he seems.
    When looked for, he is gone.
    When expected, he never shows.

    2. He practices delivery of the unseen blow.
    He fakes high while striking low.
    He distracts and hits the blind side.
    He complies, then overturns.
    Acts weak, and is suddenly strong.

FEEDING

Once an attack is launched, it can be lured along.

An incoming projectile (a fist or foot) can be
        slap-fed and pulled through as one steps aside.
The momentum can simply be "fed along"—
        helped and encouraged harmlessly along
        its path.
However, this path is now a setup, the line of
        force leading to ambush.

Any projected force (an individual or an army)
        can fall victim to "feeding."
An army that attacks can be lured deeper
        than it intends:
        falling back, feigning casualties,
        projecting an aura of weakness.
As the army or the single opponent overextends,
        close in and cut them off—
        lead them away to their graves,
        pulling them over and in,
        thus sealing their doom.

BAITING AN ATTACK

Dealt a powerful blow, the warrior suddenly collapses.

With a crumbling line of defense, an army quickly retreats.

This strategy is known as "baiting an attack."

The discerning warrior knows when to implement this
tactic, and when he himself is the intended victim
of the ruse.

By feigning serious injury, a warrior can sucker his
attacker to close in.
Seeking an easy kill, the attacker is vulnerable in
his own defense.

A retreating army can "lead" a confident attacker deep
into the wilds. Far from reinforcement, cut off
from lines of supply, the attacker grows weak and
is easily overcome.

The greatest general, the best warrior, has a keen sense
of "baiting."
He knows when it is appropriate to close in,
and when it is best to stand back.
He knows when it is time to feign weakness,
and when it is best to appear strong.

MISDIRECTION

A simple fighter will rush forward and punch
   you in the face.

A better fighter will rush forward and fake a low
   kick (which you react to), and then punch
   you in the face (left unguarded).
This fighter is on a different level: he is a
   tactician. Whereas the first fighter relies
   solely upon brute strength.

An even better fighter will not rush forward.
He may sneak in from behind and work his
   way closer. Before you know it, you're out
   cold on the floor.
Or he may appear benign. He doesn't want
   any trouble. He may even laugh and slap you
   playfully upon the back—followed by a sudden,
   twisting uppercut to the chin.

Dirty-fighting is the byword for "whatever it takes."
Though abhorred by traditionalists who have
      honorable "rules of engagement," it is increasingly
      popular with outnumbered rebels who must resort
      to guerrilla tactics.

The best warrior is aware of "misdirection"—applying
      this tactic when appropriate, or merely sensing
      when he himself is its target.

FEIGNING INJURY

A mother grouse with a broken wing will lead

   intruders away from her young. Squawking

   and fluttering helplessly, she lures them away

   from her nest. When far enough she suddenly

   bursts into flight, leaving her pursuers dumbfounded

   and frustrated.

In a similar manner, a leader can divert hostile forces

   wherever he pleases.

He can divide armies, trap and ambush, or lure

   enemies out from their stronghold.

Feigning weakness can thus tempt the strong into

   flaunting their might.

The bloody scent of an easy victory may turn

   out to be the backwind of their own defeat.

PLAYING DEAD

At certain times, against certain opponents,
      it may be necessary to play the corpse:
      to act as though one were unconscious
      or dead.

If one is being beaten senseless, if one
      cannot even begin to recover before
      another battering, a tactic of last resort
      is to feign unconsciousness.

In nature, many predators will only attack a
      live, struggling opponent.
If the prey has been killed or immobilized,
      there is nothing more to gain.
The attack is broken off as the animal loses
      interest in its victim.

In such a manner, survival may sometimes depend
      upon giving in to an overpowering opponent.
When he turns away, when one has regained
      one's senses, when one's forces have
      regrouped—then, and only then, may be
      the time for attack.

Temporary surrender is not necessarily cowardice
      if one survives with full intent to fight
      another day.

BE WARY OF SHOWING MERCY

Since a losing opponent may merely appear "down,"

the warrior must guard against this ruse.

Showing mercy may be one's downfall——do so only

with caution.

Turning away may simply provide a target

for the "knife in the back."

Not wishing to beat someone already fallen

may allow him to notch an arrow

"from the grave."

"Finishing off" may or may not be necessary.

But showing mercy should never be the reason

for a warrior to die.

LIGHTNING STRIKES

Before launching an attack never retract or draw

    back for added power or momentum. Doing so

    will forewarn your opponent, triggering defense

    or offense. Surprise should be your element—

    not his.

Drawing back before striking forward takes twice

    as long. The distance traveled is also twice as

    far: twice as much time and distance in which

    your attack can be foiled.

Animals know this instinctively, and so do great

    generals. Like lightning they go for the jugular,

    cutting off blood and air. No time is lost

    "preparing" for the kill.

FLEXIBILITY

If your opponent attempts to grapple—kick and punch.

If your opponent attempts to kick and punch—then
move in and grapple.

The natural tendency is to fight from one's best style.
The first move can be read and an appropriate
style used as a counter.

If your opponent is defensive—then undermine his
defense with strategic offense.

If your opponent is offensive—then lay your defensive
trap and wait.

A flexible, contrary approach is the hallmark of a true
warrior. Never play your opponent's game. In
his own style he is proficient, comfortable, and
secure. Playing into his hand is to pit power
against power. Switch-hitting causes confusion,
undermines his confidence, and leads to victory.

SPECIALIZATION

Mastery of an art requires diligent practice.
Many years are needed to develop a mere
     semblance of proficiency.

The limitation is time.
Only a few arts can truly be mastered in a
     lifetime. And yet each has its drawbacks
     and can be undermined by a different approach.

Being confined to one system leaves one vulnerable
     to other methods.
For this reason, the supreme warrior excels in
     a variety of arts. He must familiarize himself
     with as many skills and weapons as possible.

The training required for all-around mastery is thus
     never-ending. The knowledge required is
     inexhaustible. The task is awesome. The path
     is long and arduous. And yet, it is nevertheless
     the warrior's chosen way.

The greatest warrior is thus a generalist who
     specializes in everything. He has a broad
     mastery of virtually every aspect of war.

NATURAL ABILITIES

Because each man has his strength and weakness,

    the commander deploys his forces to advantage.

The noisy and clumsy are used for distraction

    while the stealthy are allowed to quietly slip by.

The aggressive and boisterous smash the front line

    while the lithe and agile scale the walls from behind.

The intimidating and powerful press forward on the ground

    while the skilled shoot arrows and catapults from afar.

In this way one's weakness is diminished

    while one's strength is enhanced.

BURNT BRIDGES

A bridge that has been burnt can only be rebuilt

    with great effort.

A bridge left standing can be recrossed at any time.

The enemy, however, can cross a standing bridge

    in pursuit.

To leave a bridge open for the enemy may be a

    tactical loss.

The warrior, being the ultimate tactician, must

    therefore calculate the risk of gain or loss.

Does the option of a quick retreat

    outweigh the danger of enemy pursuit?

Will bridge-burning strand one on the

    opposite shore without hope of return?

NO TURNING BACK

On the other hand . . .

Bridge-burning can be the ultimate symbolic gesture.

It says to the troops (and to the enemy):

There is no turning back.

From this point, there will be no retreat.

The courage necessary to burn a bridge can be

      empowering to the strong.

It can also be dismaying and disheartening

      to the weak.

THE BRIDGE OF TIME

A famous warlord made a controversial practice
        of burning bridges behind him. By cutting
        his own line of supply, he forced his troops
        to conquer new territory or die. The psychology
worked. The ruthless invaders stormed the
countryside taking whatever they needed. They
bred and intermingled with the indigenous
people. Generation after generation they
conquered and settled the vast, new land. They
built fortresses and raised families. Their
country became powerful and great.

Hundreds of years later this new country was itself
        invaded. After much fighting and bloodshed
        the crests of the vanquished invaders were
        displayed as trophies. But they seemed vaguely
        familiar—altered by generations—the emblems
        were discovered to be a modern variation of
        their own.

Historians puzzle over the significance of this
        fateful encounter.
In the long-run are we all not merely battling
        ourself?

PART FOUR

EULOGIES

"Only a warrior is truly prepared to greet

Death. For, to him, life itself is simply

one long wake—his own."

THE CHALLENGE

The warrior awakens with a needling sense that

something is wrong. He checks his mat, his

possessions, his surroundings. Nothing

appears to be amiss. And yet . . .

The sensation persists—an unidentifiable

discomfort.

He dons armor and weapons to ward off the

irritation. He feels better fortified—

and yet things are still not right.

The warrior turns both inward and outward.

Slowly and warily he circles the room. He

seeks the source of the disruption. He finds

it everywhere—and yet nowhere. He must

prepare for battle against an invisible foe.

THE PREPARATION

The warrior centers himself—

    calms the disturbance within so as to

    identify the disturbance without.

His mind becomes a pristine mirror to reflect

    all distortions.

The sword at his side has not yet been drawn—

    has not even been touched—

    has never been given a thought.

The void cannot echo until there has been a shout.

THE RESPONSE

A shout resounds through the void (was it the

warrior's own?).

The echo reverberates.

The sword is drawn in a flash,

flashing with blinding, polished brilliance

as it poises on-guard.

The slightest movement will trigger a slashing

response.

The vaguest threat will be dispatched immediately—

mercilessly.

THE CUT

A slight movement, perhaps only a breeze,

triggers the response.

The diamond blade slices the icy air in a

moment frozen in time.

Eternity is laid bare to the bone.

THE RETURN

The essence is wiped clean.

The sword is withdrawn and replaced in its sheath.

Stillness reverberates.

Silence rings in the ears.

Balance and harmony have been restored.

The universe is once more at peace.

ENDGAME

As the battle draws to a close,

    the wins and losses are tallied up.

One may be a winner or a loser,

    but the war is over.

There is nothing more to be done.

It was, after all, only a game.

The pieces are set aside.

One is ready to go home.

One feels a sense of loss,

    and yet of completion.

One feels tired,

    and yet at peace.

DOING ONE'S BEST

The true warrior rests assured that he has done his best.

It was a difficult battle,

    but whether victor or conquered,

        it is now time to return home.

He has no regrets,

    for it was his chosen way.

To the accomplished warrior the results of the battle

    are secondary.

What is primary is his conduct and the integrity of

    his fight.

THE FINAL ACT

The warrior's way is one of performance.

It is the rehearsal as well as the last show.

It is the debut as well as the final take.

Every movement is witnessed.

Each action is recorded for all time.

In the end, the warrior's life was his art—

    immortalized with the last stroke

        as the curtains fall . . .

CURTAIN CALL

And now that all has been said and done,

    the Master appears as one returns one's sword.

Death awaits, off to the side,

    applauding one's last bows.

No finer audience could have been hoped for,

    no more enthusiastic a fan.

Death, one's friend and lover,

    is ready to consummate the final act.

NIGHTFALL

The applause dies.

The music fades.

The golden glow of sunset is softened by twilight.

The warrior relinquishes his command to the dark

sentinels of the night.

All the fanfare of the past is a mere echo of memory.

All the skirmishes and intrigue are little more than

a brief thought.

Darkness envelopes the battlefield.

The dead cannot be distinguished from those who sleep.

A DEATHLY DREAM

The phantom warrior sits astride his ghostly, white steed.

The dead stand at attention as one more joins their ranks.

It was his chosen way of life—

    a life of living Death.

And now Death has been honored as the warrior seals

    his pact.

Was it merely a dream?

    all that went before . . .

Was life only in his mind?

With Death, the warrior's awakening has finally been

    achieved.

AWAKENING

All wars are ultimately lost.

And yet, all battles have been won.

The true warrior never loses so long as his soul

remains intact.

Mistakes are a part of life—wrong turns—bad choices.

However, if the intention was sincere,

the warrior is never far off course.

He dies at peace, and without regret.

FATE

As a condemned prisoner facing execution,

    the warrior moves through life,

    gracefully accepting his allotted fate.

Death smiles kindly at the return of his prodigal son.

After all the commotion and endless chatter,

    the youthful dalliance and intrigue,

    the weary vagabond finds his way home at last.

THE ULTIMATE SURRENDER

All struggling finally ceases.

No more victories are to be gained.

The heated action cools as Death adjudicates surrender.

The wheel, having turned, at last comes to rest.